Hairy, Scary, Ordinary

What Is an Adjective?

adjective: A word that describes a thing, idea, or living being.

Hairy, Scary, Ordinary

What Is an Adjective?

by Brian P. Cleary

illustrated by Jenya Prosmitsky

M MILLBROOK PRESS / MINNEAPOLIS

Adjectives are words like hairy,

Scary, cool, and ordinary.

They tell us
things
are
orange
or
green,

Hot or cold or in-between,

Adjectives help tell us more,

Like narrow street or favorite store,

Hilly, chilly, fast, and fun, undercooked and overdone.

They tell us of an old black boot,

A rainy day, a wrinkled suit,

A silly
teacher,
giant
hair,

A large cow
at the local fair—

Kickballs that are red and rubber,

Spot's clean fur each time you scrub her,

Cold, dark mornings,

hot pink shades,

Young girls drinking lemonades.

They tell if root beer's *flat or fizzy*,

And if your street is *quiet* or *busy*,

That treats
are yummy,

shakes are
thick,

And if your
tummy's calm
or sick.

They're colorful, like mauve and puce,

They help explain, like lean and loose,

Baggy, saggy, stretchy, strong,

Much too short or way too long.

Frilly,
silly,

polka-dotted,

single-looped

or

double-knotted.

Words like
Spunky,

rather
clunky,

Priceless, nice,

NOT FOR SALE

or downright junky,

Speedy, Spoiled,

Spiffy, Spare,

Thrifty, nifty

bronze and bare.

·THE FOOT · MICHELANGEL·TOE·

They **modify** nouns
in ways that help tell us

If
someone's
sincere,

delighted, or **jealous,**

If jackets are herringbone,
pinstriped, or plaid,

If babies
are

crabby, excited, or glad.

They
tell us
that
shows
are stupid or funny,

of books that
are stuffy,
amazing, or punny,

of looks that are frightening,

dogs that are stray,

of coffee that's black
in a cup
that is gray.

Adjectives help us describe when we're **tired,**

Or say when we're grumpy,

or when we are **Wired.**

Lopsided, one-sided ball games that bore us,

The sweet, gentle sounds that descend from the chorus,

So, what is an **adjective?**

Do you know?

ABOUT THE AUTHOR & ILLUSTRATOR

BRIAN P. CLEARY is the author of several other picture books, including <u>Rainbow Soup: Adventures in Poetry</u> and <u>Peanut Butter and Jellyfishes: A Very Silly Alphabet Book</u>. He lives in Cleveland, Ohio.

JENYA PROSMITSKY grew up and studied art in Chisinau, Moldova. Her two cats, Henry and Freddy, were vital to her illustrations for this book.

This book is available in two editions:
Library binding by Millbrook Press, Inc., a division of Lerner Publishing Group
Soft cover by First Avenue Editions, an imprint of Lerner Publishing Group
241 First Avenue North, Minneapolis, MN 55401 U.S.A.

Website address: www.lernerbooks.com

Library of Congress Cataloging-in-Publication Data

Cleary, Brian P., 1959-
    Hairy, scary, ordinary : what is an adjective? / Brian P. Cleary ;
illustrated by Jenya Prosmitsky.
      p. cm. — (Words are categorical)
    Summary: Rhyming text and illustrations of comical cats present numerous examples of adjectives, from "hairy, scary, cool, and ordinary" to "tan and tall," "funny, frisky, smooth, and small."
    ISBN-13: 978-1-57505-401-8 (lib. bdg. : alk. paper)
    ISBN-10: 1-57505-401-9 (lib. bdg. : alk. paper)
    ISBN-13: 978-1-57505-554-1 (pbk. : alk. paper)
    ISBN-10: 1-57505-554-6 (pbk. : alk. paper)
    1. English language—Adjective—Juvenile literature. [1. English language—Adjective.] I. Prosmitsky, Jenya, 1974- ill. II. Title. III. Series: Cleary, Brian P., 1959- Words are categorical.
PE1241.C57 1999   98-32132
428.2—dc21

Manufactured in the United States of America
11 12 13 14 15 16 - JR - 11 10 09 08 07 06